RICK WAR... D0401400

THE
MIRACLE
OF MERCY

A Six-Session Video-Based
Study for Small Groups

> *"Blessed are the merciful, for they will be shown mercy."*
> **MATTHEW 5:7 (NIV)**

THE MIRACLE OF MERCY

Small Group Study Guide
Edition 1.0 — Special Edition for Saddleback Church Small Groups
Copyright © 2016 Saddleback Church

Requests for information should be addressed to:
Saddleback Resources
30021 Comercio
Rancho Santa Margarita, CA 92688

ISBN: 978-1-4228-0400-1

Scripture quotations noted CEV are from The Contemporary English Version.
Copyright © 1991, 1992, 1995 by American Bible Society. Used by permission.

Scripture quotations noted ESV are from The Holy Bible, English Standard Version®
(ESV®). Copyright © 2001 by Crossway, a publishing ministry of Good News
Publishers. Used by permission. All rights reserved.

Scripture quotations noted GW are from God's Word. Copyright © 1995
by God's Word to the Nations Bible Society. Used by permission. All rights reserved.

Scripture quotations noted KJV are from The King James Version.

Scripture quotations noted MSG are from The Message. Copyright © by Eugene H.
Peterson, 1993, 1994, 1995, 1996, 2000, 2001, 2002. Used by permission of NavPress
Publishing Group. All rights reserved.

Scripture quotations noted NCV are from The Holy Bible, New Century Version.
Copyright © 1987, 1988, 1991 by Word Publishing, a division of Thomas Nelson, Inc.
Used by permission. All rights reserved.

Scriptures quotations noted NIV are from THE HOLY BIBLE, NEW INTERNATIONAL
VERSION®, NIV®. Copyright © 1973, 1978, 1984, 2011 by International Bible Society.
Used by permission of Zondervan. All rights reserved.

Scriptures quotations noted NLT are taken from The Holy Bible, New Living
Translation, Second Edition. Copyright © 1996, 2005 by Tyndale House Publishers,
Inc., Wheaton, IL 60189. All rights reserved.

Scriptures quotations noted NKJV are taken from the New King James Version.
Copyright © 1979, 1980, 1982 by Thomas Nelson, Inc. Used by permission.
All rights reserved.

Printed and bound in the United States of America.

CONTENTS

Blessed are the merciful, for they will be shown mercy.

MATTHEW 5:7
(NIV)

WELCOME TO
THE MIRACLE OF MERCY

Did you know that mercy is God's number one characteristic in the Bible? More than his sovereignty, omniscience, omnipotence, omnipresence, or any other fancy words about him—more than anything else, the number one attribute of God in Scripture is his mercy.

The world portrays God as a God of anger and judgment. But God shows himself first and foremost as a God of mercy. All the way back when God revealed his glory to Moses and gave him the Ten Commandments, God said, "This is my name: *The Lord, the Lord God, merciful and gracious, longsuffering, and abounding in goodness and truth*" (Exodus 34:6 NKJV). Notice his number one characteristic is mercy. God did not say, "I am the Lord God, just and righteous," or "The Lord God, eternal and all powerful." He said, "This is who I am. I am merciful, gracious, patient, overflowing with kindness, goodness, faithfulness, and truth."

If mercy is God's number one characteristic that he reveals to us in the Bible—if that is the most important thing he wants us to know about him—then it must be the most important thing for us to *learn* about him. And it must also be the most important character trait that God wants to develop in us. God is merciful, and he wants us to be merciful too.

We are going to spend the next six sessions learning what God's mercy is all about. In the first session, I will introduce the five marks of mercy: mercy forgives the fallen, helps the hurting, is patient with difficult people, is kind to enemies, and cares for the lost. In each of the following sessions, we will explore more deeply these facets of mercy and see how they apply to our lives.

The Bible says we are to be not just hearers of the Word, but also doers of the Word. So in each session, you will find suggestions for how you can put these truths into practice both on a personal level and as a small group. At the end of each session, you will also find Bible verses and journal pages for your daily devotions. I encourage you to take five minutes each day to read the verses and talk to God about them.

Jesus said, *"Blessed are the merciful, for they will be shown mercy."* Let's take the next forty days to see what mercy really looks like.

Pastor Rick

Pastor Rick

HOW TO USE THIS STUDY GUIDE

Here is a brief explanation of the features of this study guide.

- **Checking In:** Open each meeting by briefly discussing a question or two that will help focus everyone's attention on the subject of the lesson.

- **Memory Verse:** Each week you will find a key Bible verse for your group to memorize together. If someone in the group has a different translation, ask them to read it aloud so the group can get a bigger picture of the meaning of the passage.

- **Video Lesson:** There is a video lesson for the group to watch together each week. Fill in the blanks in the lesson outlines as you watch the video, and be sure to refer back to these outlines during your discussion time.

- **Discovery Questions:** Each video segment is complemented by several questions for group discussion. Please don't feel pressured to discuss every single question. There is no reason to rush through the answers. Give everyone ample opportunity to share their thoughts. If you don't get through all of the discovery questions, that's okay.

- **Putting It into Practice:** This is where the rubber meets the road. We don't want to be just hearers of the Word. We also need to be doers of the Word (James 1:22). These assignments are application exercises that will help you put into practice the truths you have discussed in the lesson. There is a personal application and a group application in each session.

- **Diving Deeper:** This section contains directions for your group members' daily devotions.

- **Prayer Direction:** At the end of each session, you will find suggestions for your group prayer time. Praying together is one of the greatest privileges of small group life. Please don't take it for granted.

- **Daily Devotions and Journal Pages:** There are seven daily devotions and seven journal pages at the end of each session in your study guide. Use these for your daily quiet times throughout the week.

- **Small Group Resources:** There are additional small group resources, such as *Small Group Guidelines, Helps for Hosts, Small Group Prayer* and *Praise Reports*, etc., in the back of this study guide.

A TIP FOR THE HOST

The study guide material is meant to be your servant, not your master. The point is not to race through the sessions; the point is to take time to let God work in your lives. It is not necessary to "go around the circle" before you move on to the next question. Give people the freedom to speak, but don't insist on it. Your group will enjoy deeper, more open sharing and discussion if people don't feel pressured to speak up.

THE FIVE MARKS OF MERCY

CHECKING IN

- If this is your group's first meeting, or if you have any new group members, be sure to introduce yourselves. Before you begin this study, review the *Small Group Guidelines* on page 153 of this study guide.

- What does mercy mean to you?

MEMORY VERSE

"Blessed are the merciful, for they will be shown mercy."

MATTHEW 5:7 (NIV)

WATCH THE VIDEO LESSON NOW AND FOLLOW ALONG IN YOUR OUTLINE.

THE FIVE MARKS OF MERCY

Did you know God's mercy is his number one characteristic in the Bible? More than his sovereignty, omniscience, omnipotence, omnipresence, or any other fancy words about him—more than his anger or justice or judgment—more than anything else, the number one attribute of God in Scripture is his mercy.

> *The Lord, the Lord God, merciful and gracious, longsuffering, and abounding in goodness and truth.*
>
> **EXODUS 34:6 (NKJV)**

- Mercy is <u>LOVE</u> in <u>ACTION</u>.

MERCY: *refraining from harm or punishment; unexpected kindness*

> *The Lord is merciful and compassionate, slow to get angry and filled with unfailing love.*
>
> **PSALM 145:8 (NLT[2005])**

THE FIVE MARKS OF MERCY

- I <u>FORGIVE</u> those who have <u>FALLEN</u>.

> *Be gentle and ready to forgive; never hold grudges. Remember, the Lord forgave you, so you must forgive others.*
>
> **COLOSSIANS 3:13 (TLB)**

> *Mercy triumphs over judgment.*
>
> **JAMES 2:13b (NIV)**

- I __HELP__ those who are __HURTING__ .

Suppose a brother or sister is without clothes and daily food. If one of you says to him, "Go, I wish you well; keep warm and well fed," but does nothing about his physical needs, what good is it? In the same way, faith by itself, if it is not accompanied by action, is dead.

JAMES 2:15–17 (NIV)

As Christ's followers, our faith is merciful to its core. Mercy takes action where others take off.

Whenever you possibly can, do good to those who need it.

PROVERBS 3:27 (TEV)

Mercy is not theoretical or philosophical. Mercy is practical. Mercy isn't something you just talk about. It's something you do! Mercy gets its hands dirty.

If someone who is supposed to be a Christian has enough money to live well, and sees a brother in need, and won't help him—how can God's love be within him? . . . Let us stop just saying we love people; let us really love them, and show it by our actions.

1 JOHN 3:17–18 (TLB)

- I am __PATIENT__ with difficult people.

Encourage the timid, help the weak, be patient with everyone.

1 THESSALONIANS 5:14b (NIV)

There's a hurt behind every hang-up. There's a twist in every story.

Accept each other just as Christ has accepted you.

ROMANS 15:7 (NLT)

It's a lot easier to criticize than to sympathize. It's a lot easier to point a finger than to lend a helping hand. But merciful people are not quick to criticize or judge.

- I am __KIND__ to my __ENEMIES__ .

"If you do good to those who do good to you, what credit is that to you? Even 'sinners' do that . . . But love your enemies, do good to them . . . Then your reward will be great, and you will be sons of the Most High, because he is kind to the ungrateful and wicked."

LUKE 6:33, 35 (NIV)

- I __CARE__ for the __LOST__ .

For God so loved the world that He gave His only begotten Son, that whoever believes in Him should not perish but have everlasting life.

JOHN 3:16 (NKJV)

Mercy does all it can to keep people from going to hell. The greatest act of mercy you can do is to share the Good News of Jesus Christ.

THREE MOTIVATIONS FOR MERCY

- **I must be merciful because __GOD IS MERCIFUL__ .**

The Lord is kind and does what is right; our God is merciful.

PSALM 116:5 (NCV)

"Be merciful, just as your Father is merciful."

LUKE 6:36 (NIV)

At one time you were far away from God and were his enemies because of the evil things you did and thought. But now, by means of the physical death of his Son, God has made you his friends.

COLOSSIANS 1:21–22 (TEV)

- **I must be merciful because** _I NEED MERCY EVERYDAY_ .

No mercy will be shown to those who show no mercy to others.

JAMES 2:13 (GW)

"Blessed are the merciful, for they will be shown mercy."

MATTHEW 5:7 (NIV)

Mercy is a two-way street. When you refuse to show mercy to others, you're burning the very bridge you have to walk across to receive God's mercy yourself.

- **I must be merciful because** _MERCY MAKES ME HAPPY_ .

Your own soul is nourished when you are kind; it is destroyed when you are cruel.

PROVERBS 11:17 (TLB)

DISCOVERY QUESTIONS

Please don't feel pressured to discuss every discovery question. It's okay to choose the questions that are right for your group. The point is not to race through the session; the point is to take time to let God work in your lives.

- Mercy is God's number one characteristic in the Bible. How does that truth affect the way you think about God?

- How does God's mercy affect the way you think about others?

- Which of the five marks of mercy is the most challenging for you?

- Share a time when someone showed mercy to you. How did their unexpected kindness impact your life?

PUTTING IT INTO PRACTICE

This is where the rubber meets the road. We don't want to be just hearers of the Word. We also need to be doers of the Word (James 1:22). These assignments are application exercises that will help you put into practice the truths you have discussed in the lesson. There is a personal application and a group application in each session.

PERSONAL

What opportunity do you have to show mercy to someone this week? Does someone need your forgiveness? Does someone need your compassion? How about your patience or kindness? Do you know someone who doesn't know Jesus? Choose one of the five marks of mercy and answer these questions. Be specific.

- Who will it be? _____

- What will I do? _____

- When will I do it? _____

- Where will I do it? _____

- How will I do it? _____

GROUP

We don't want to be just hearers of the Word. We must be doers of the Word. The Bible says, *"Faith that does nothing is worth nothing"* (James 2:20b NCV). What can your group do to show God's mercy to someone in need? During this *Miracle of Mercy* study, we are encouraging every small group to serve together in what we're calling Mercy Projects. These projects provide simple, practical ways for you and your group to show Christ's love and mercy to people in your community. Here are your first steps:

- Talk with your group about the Mercy Project assignment. For a list of serving ideas and opportunities, visit *saddleback.com/ mercyprojects*. You don't have to make a final choice today. Just talk about the options. You can make your final project decision next week.

- Identify a Mercy Project champion in your small group. The champion does not have to do all the work. Their job is to gather information on three optional projects from the website this week, and help coordinate the selection and completion of your service project in the weeks to come.

- Agree with your group that between now and your next session, you will all pray about which Mercy Project to take on.

DIVING DEEPER

Miracle of Mercy Daily Devotions. On pages 20–33, you will find Bible verses about mercy, along with prompts for journaling your thoughts. Make the commitment with your group that you will give at least five minutes every day this week to read and meditate on these verses. Follow the prompts and write down your responses.

PRAYER DIRECTION

We recommend that larger groups break into subgroups of three or four people for prayer. If you are a coed group, subgroup by gender. This will give everyone ample time to share and pray together. If praying in a group is new or uncomfortable for you, we encourage you to start by praying single sentence prayers. Don't worry about how fancy you sound. God isn't looking for eloquence. He just wants honesty. Talk to God like you talk to a friend. Give everyone a chance to pray, but don't insist on it. Over time, you will all feel much more comfortable praying together.

- If you prayed with Pastor Rick at the end of his message and opened your life to Jesus Christ, be sure to tell your group and let them celebrate your decision with you. Visit *saddleback.com/ freshstart* for free resources to help you get started in your new life in Christ.

- Break into smaller groups of two or three and pray for each other about the personal steps you wrote down in the *Putting It into Practice* section. Ask God to help you be merciful this week.

- Ask God to show you how he would like your group to serve in a Mercy Project.

- Share your prayer requests with your group and pray for each other. Be sure to record your prayer requests on the *Small Group Prayer* and *Praise Report* on page 156 of your study guide.

BEFORE YOU GO

Healthy groups share responsibilities and group ownership. Turn to the *Small Group Calendar* on page 158 of this study guide. Fill out the calendar together, at least for next week, noting where you will meet each week, who will facilitate your meeting, and who will provide a meal or snack. Note special events, socials, or days off as well. Your Group Host will be very appreciative, and everyone will have a lot more fun together. This would be a great role for someone to coordinate for the group.

Collect basic contact information, such as phone numbers and email addresses, for your group members. The *Group Roster* on page 161 of your study guide is a good place to record this information.

THE FIVE MARKS OF MERCY

Read this Scripture passage several times, slowly. Emphasize a different word or phrase each time you read the passage. Underline keywords or phrases that are especially meaningful to you. Then take a few minutes to write your thoughts on the journal page. Finish with a prayer.

Blessed are the merciful, for they will be shown mercy.

MATTHEW 5:7 (NIV)

WHAT DID YOU HEAR?

What did God say to you as you read today's Bible passage? What word or phrase was most meaningful to you?

WHAT DO YOU THINK?

What does this passage mean to you? How does it apply to your life?

WHAT WILL YOU DO?

How will you put this verse into practice?

NOW YOU PRAY

This is where you turn your thoughts into prayer. It could be a prayer of gratitude or praise. It could be a prayer of confession or a request for God's help. It's up to you. But take a minute to write a prayer of response to God.

THE FIVE MARKS OF MERCY

Read this Scripture passage several times, slowly. Emphasize a different word or phrase each time you read the passage. Underline keywords or phrases that are especially meaningful to you. Then take a few minutes to write your thoughts on the journal page. Finish with a prayer.

The Lord is merciful and compassionate, slow to get angry and filled with unfailing love.

PSALM 145:8 (NLT[2005])

WHAT DID YOU HEAR?

What did God say to you as you read today's Bible passage? What word or phrase was most meaningful to you?

WHAT DO YOU THINK?

What does this passage mean to you? How does it apply to your life?

WHAT WILL YOU DO?

How will you put this verse into practice?

NOW YOU PRAY

This is where you turn your thoughts into prayer. It could be a prayer of gratitude or praise. It could be a prayer of confession or a request for God's help. It's up to you. But take a minute to write a prayer of response to God.

THE FIVE MARKS OF MERCY

Read this Scripture passage several times, slowly. Emphasize a different word or phrase each time you read the passage. Underline keywords or phrases that are especially meaningful to you. Then take a few minutes to write your thoughts on the journal page. Finish with a prayer.

Be gentle and ready to forgive; never hold grudges. Remember, the Lord forgave you, so you must forgive others.

COLOSSIANS 3:13 (TLB)

WHAT DID YOU HEAR?

What did God say to you as you read today's Bible passage? What word or phrase was most meaningful to you?

WHAT DO YOU THINK?

What does this passage mean to you? How does it apply to your life?

WHAT WILL YOU DO?

How will you put this verse into practice?

NOW YOU PRAY

This is where you turn your thoughts into prayer. It could be a prayer of gratitude or praise. It could be a prayer of confession or a request for God's help. It's up to you. But take a minute to write a prayer of response to God.

THE FIVE MARKS OF MERCY

Read this Scripture passage several times, slowly. Emphasize a different word or phrase each time you read the passage. Underline keywords or phrases that are especially meaningful to you. Then take a few minutes to write your thoughts on the journal page. Finish with a prayer.

Suppose a brother or sister is without clothes and daily food. If one of you says to him, *"Go, I wish you well; keep warm and well fed,"* but does nothing about his physical needs, what good is it? In the same way, faith by itself, if it is not accompanied by action, is dead.

JAMES 2:15–17 (NIV)

WHAT DID YOU HEAR?

What did God say to you as you read today's Bible passage? What word or phrase was most meaningful to you?

WHAT DO YOU THINK?

What does this passage mean to you? How does it apply to your life?

WHAT WILL YOU DO?

How will you put this verse into practice?

NOW YOU PRAY

This is where you turn your thoughts into prayer. It could be a prayer of gratitude or praise. It could be a prayer of confession or a request for God's help. It's up to you. But take a minute to write a prayer of response to God.

THE FIVE MARKS OF MERCY

Read this Scripture passage several times, slowly. Emphasize a different word or phrase each time you read the passage. Underline keywords or phrases that are especially meaningful to you. Then take a few minutes to write your thoughts on the journal page. Finish with a prayer.

Whenever you possibly can, do good to those who need it.

PROVERBS 3:27 (TEV)

WHAT DID YOU HEAR?
What did God say to you as you read today's Bible passage? What word or phrase was most meaningful to you?

WHAT DO YOU THINK?
What does this passage mean to you? How does it apply to your life?

WHAT WILL YOU DO?
How will you put this verse into practice?

NOW YOU PRAY
This is where you turn your thoughts into prayer. It could be a prayer of gratitude or praise. It could be a prayer of confession or a request for God's help. It's up to you. But take a minute to write a prayer of response to God.

THE FIVE MARKS OF MERCY

Read this Scripture passage several times, slowly. Emphasize a different word or phrase each time you read the passage. Underline keywords or phrases that are especially meaningful to you. Then take a few minutes to write your thoughts on the journal page. Finish with a prayer.

Encourage the timid,
help the weak, be patient
with everyone.

1 THESSALONIANS 5:14b (NIV)

WHAT DID YOU HEAR?

What did God say to you as you read today's Bible passage? What word or phrase was most meaningful to you?

WHAT DO YOU THINK?

What does this passage mean to you? How does it apply to your life?

WHAT WILL YOU DO?

How will you put this verse into practice?

NOW YOU PRAY

This is where you turn your thoughts into prayer. It could be a prayer of gratitude or praise. It could be a prayer of confession or a request for God's help. It's up to you. But take a minute to write a prayer of response to God.

THE FIVE MARKS OF MERCY

Read this Scripture passage several times, slowly. Emphasize a different word or phrase each time you read the passage. Underline keywords or phrases that are especially meaningful to you. Then take a few minutes to write your thoughts on the journal page. Finish with a prayer.

"If you do good to those who do good to you, what credit is that to you? Even 'sinners' do that ... But love your enemies, do good to them ... Then your reward will be great, and you will be sons of the Most High, because he is kind to the ungrateful and wicked."

LUKE 6:33, 35 (NIV)

WHAT DID YOU HEAR?

What did God say to you as you read today's Bible passage? What word or phrase was most meaningful to you?

WHAT DO YOU THINK?

What does this passage mean to you? How does it apply to your life?

WHAT WILL YOU DO?

How will you put this verse into practice?

NOW YOU PRAY

This is where you turn your thoughts into prayer. It could be a prayer of gratitude or praise. It could be a prayer of confession or a request for God's help. It's up to you. But take a minute to write a prayer of response to God.

MERCY FORGIVES THE FALLEN

SESSION TWO

CHECKING IN

Choose one of these ideas to start your session.

- Share a verse that was especially meaningful to you in your *Miracle of Mercy Daily Devotions* this past week.

- In our last session, you identified a personal opportunity to show mercy. Would any of you like to share your experience with putting your plan into action?

MEMORY VERSE

Love keeps no record of wrongs.

1 CORINTHIANS 13:5b (NIV)

 WATCH THE VIDEO LESSON NOW AND FOLLOW ALONG IN YOUR OUTLINE.

MERCY FORGIVES THE FALLEN

Peter came to Jesus and asked, "Lord, how many times shall I forgive my brother when he sins against me? Up to seven times?"

MATTHEW 18:21 (NIV)

It's the people you know best who are able to hurt you the most deeply and the most often.

"Not seven times, but seventy-seven times."

MATTHEW 18:22b (NIV)

If you're keeping score, then you're missing the point. If you're counting, then it doesn't count.

"The servant fell on his knees before him. 'Be patient with me,' he begged, 'and I will pay back everything.'"

MATTHEW 18:26 (NIV)

THREE REASONS I MUST LEARN TO FORGIVE

- **Because** _____.

"The servant's master took pity on him, canceled the debt and let him go."

MATTHEW 18:27 (NIV)

"But when that servant went out, he found one of his fellow servants who owed him a hundred denarii. He grabbed him and began to choke him. 'Pay back what you owe me!' he demanded. His fellow servant fell to his knees and begged him, 'Be patient with me, and I will pay you back.' But he refused. Instead, he went off and had the man thrown into prison until he could pay the debt."

MATTHEW 18:28–30 (NIV)

God has forgiven me an impossible debt! He has forgiven my sins, and now he expects me to forgive other people.

> *Be kind and compassionate to one another, forgiving each other, just as in Christ God forgave you.*
>
> EPHESIANS 4:32 (NIV)

- **Because** _____

  _____ .

> *"When the other servants saw what had happened, they were greatly distressed and went and told their master everything that had happened. Then the master called the servant in. 'You wicked servant,' he said, 'I canceled all that debt of yours because you begged me to. Shouldn't you have had mercy on your fellow servant just as I had on you?' In anger his master turned him over to the jailers to be tortured, until he should pay back all he owed."*
>
> MATTHEW 18:31–34 (NIV)

The servant was not tortured because of his debt. He was tortured because of his unforgiveness!

> *Some people . . . die happy and at ease . . . Others have no happiness at all; they live and die with bitter hearts.*
>
> JOB 21:23–25 (TEV)

The torture chamber of unforgiveness is self-imposed. When we fail to forgive, God doesn't have to lock us up in jail. We do it to ourselves. We lock ourselves in a jail of anger and anxiety.

- **Because** _____ **in the future.**

> *"This is how my heavenly Father will treat each of you unless you forgive your brother from your heart."*
>
> MATTHEW 18:35 (NIV)

"Blessed are the merciful, for they will be shown mercy."

MATTHEW 5:7 (NIV)

Forgiveness is not lip service; forgiveness is a way of life. We have to live in a constant state of forgiveness—accepting God's forgiveness and offering forgiveness to others—no matter how many times they sin against us.

Forgiveness is not the instant restoration of trust. Not at all. Forgiveness— letting go—is instant. But trust must be rebuilt over time.

> *Never avenge yourselves. Leave that to God, for he has said that he will repay those who deserve it.*

ROMANS 12:19 (TLB)

Who do you think can do a better job of straightening out the other person, you or God?

> *Love keeps no record of wrongs.*

1 CORINTHIANS 13:5b (NIV)

Are you keeping score of somebody's sins against you? Have they reached "seven" yet? How about seventy-seven? What if God kept score against you? Because of the cross, God keeps no record of your wrongs against him; and because of the cross, he expects you to keep no record of the wrongs that have been done against you.

Now you might say, "It wouldn't be fair to forgive that person. After all they've done to me, it's just not fair." And you're right. It isn't fair. But forgiveness is not about fairness. Forgiveness is about grace. Is it fair that God forgave you?

HOW CAN YOU RELEASE YOUR HURT?

- _____
- _____

Be careful that none of you fails to respond to the grace which God gives, for if he does there can very easily spring up in him a bitter spirit which is not only bad in itself but can also poison the lives of many others.

HEBREWS 12:15 (PH)

—————————————————————

We know that our old life died with Christ on the cross so that our sinful selves would have no power over us and we would not be slaves to sin.

ROMANS 6:6 (NCV)

Don't be a slave any longer to the sin of unforgiveness. Release your grip on the person who hurt you. Do it every day if you have to. No matter how often that painful memory returns, bring it to God, ask for his grace, and then leave your hurt at the cross.

If your group is coed, we recommend that you break into subgroups by gender to encourage openness in your discussion. This will be especially helpful in the *Putting It into Practice* and *Prayer Direction* sections of your study.

DISCOVERY QUESTIONS

- Is it difficult for you to believe that God has completely forgiven you and doesn't hold your past against you?

- How can unforgiveness toward others affect your relationship with God?

- Pastor Rick said, "Forgiveness is not about fairness. Forgiveness is about grace." How do you respond to that?

- Have you been forgiven by someone who chose grace over getting even? How did their gift of forgiveness affect your relationship with them?

PUTTING IT INTO PRACTICE

PERSONAL

As you listened to Pastor Rick's message, did the Holy Spirit bring someone to your mind that you need to forgive? If so, follow these steps.

THE FIRST STEP
Pinpoint the issue. Do you feel anxiety, anger, or bitterness toward anyone? This is a clue that you need to release that person and work on forgiveness.

THE SECOND STEP
Invite the Holy Spirit to search your heart as you read all of the verses in today's message outline. Allow the power of God's Word to penetrate your heart and mind with its truth.

THE THIRD STEP

Turn to God in prayer. Here is a prayer you can use to help you get started.

Dear Lord,

I choose today to forgive

_____ [NAME] _____.

I ask for your power to do this.

I realize trust may take time to rebuild,

but I choose to hold no grudges.

Help me to let go of bitterness and anger in my heart,

so that I may live in freedom.

Help me understand how much you have forgiven me.

Give me your grace so that I can let go of my "right" to get even.

Now, Lord, I ask you to bless this person who has hurt me.

In particular,

I ask you to bless him/her with these things:

_____

_____

_____

Now, Lord, please replace my pain with your peace.

Replace my loss with your love.

May the past truly be the past.

In Jesus' name I pray. Amen.

If you are not ready to pray that prayer yet—if the pain is just too deep—then pray, "Lord, help me to become willing to forgive."

Some hurts are so deep that it could take days or even weeks to completely let go. If the memory of that hurt comes back, repeat these steps. Do them as often as you need until you have found peace.

In our last session, we introduced the idea of your small group doing a Mercy Project together. Here are your steps for this week.

- Your Mercy Project champion should present to your group the information on three serving opportunities they gathered from *saddleback.com/mercyprojects*.

- As a group, choose one Mercy Project that works best for all of you.

- Before your next group meeting, your Mercy Project champion should work to begin scheduling your serving day. Be sure to give yourselves a deadline for action. Without a date, it's not a plan, it's just an idea.

DIVING DEEPER

Miracle of Mercy Daily Devotions. On pages 44–57, you will find Bible verses about forgiveness, along with prompts for journaling your thoughts. Make the commitment with your group that you will give at least five minutes every day this week to read and meditate on these verses. Follow the prompts and write down your responses.

PRAYER DIRECTION

- Break into subgroups of three or four people. Start your group prayer time by thanking God for his forgiveness.

- Confess to one another if you need to forgive someone. This is not a time to share details. Simply mention the person's name or the nature of the relationship (e.g., family member, colleague, neighbor, friend, etc.). Then pray for one another, asking God to soften your hearts and give you the courage and grace to forgive. If you are not yet ready to forgive that person, then pray that God will help you to become "willing to be ready."

- Pray that God will use your group to show the love of Christ to others through your group's Mercy Project.

- Share your prayer requests with your group and pray for each other. Be sure to record your prayer requests on the *Small Group Prayer and Praise Report* on page 156 of your study guide.

MERCY FORGIVES THE FALLEN

Read this Scripture passage several times, slowly. Emphasize a different word or phrase each time you read the passage. Underline keywords or phrases that are especially meaningful to you. Then take a few minutes to write your thoughts on the journal page. Finish with a prayer.

Love keeps no record of wrongs.

1 CORINTHIANS 13:5b (NIV)

WHAT DID YOU HEAR?

What did God say to you as you read today's Bible passage? What word or phrase was most meaningful to you?

WHAT DO YOU THINK?

What does this passage mean to you? How does it apply to your life?

WHAT WILL YOU DO?

How will you put this verse into practice?

NOW YOU PRAY

This is where you turn your thoughts into prayer. It could be a prayer of gratitude or praise. It could be a prayer of confession or a request for God's help. It's up to you. But take a minute to write a prayer of response to God.

MERCY FORGIVES THE FALLEN

Read this Scripture passage several times, slowly. Emphasize a different word or phrase each time you read the passage. Underline keywords or phrases that are especially meaningful to you. Then take a few minutes to write your thoughts on the journal page. Finish with a prayer.

Peter came to Jesus and asked, "Lord, how many times shall I forgive my brother when he sins against me? Up to seven times?" Jesus answered, *"I tell you, not seven times, but seventy-seven times."*

MATTHEW 18:21–22 (NIV)

WHAT DID YOU HEAR?

What did God say to you as you read today's Bible passage? What word or phrase was most meaningful to you?

WHAT DO YOU THINK?

What does this passage mean to you? How does it apply to your life?

WHAT WILL YOU DO?

How will you put this verse into practice?

NOW YOU PRAY

This is where you turn your thoughts into prayer. It could be a prayer of gratitude or praise. It could be a prayer of confession or a request for God's help. It's up to you. But take a minute to write a prayer of response to God.

MERCY FORGIVES THE FALLEN

Read this Scripture passage several times, slowly. Emphasize a different word or phrase each time you read the passage. Underline keywords or phrases that are especially meaningful to you. Then take a few minutes to write your thoughts on the journal page. Finish with a prayer.

Be kind and compassionate to one another, forgiving each other, just as in Christ God forgave you.

EPHESIANS 4:32 (NIV)

WHAT DID YOU HEAR?

What did God say to you as you read today's Bible passage? What word or phrase was most meaningful to you?

WHAT DO YOU THINK?

What does this passage mean to you? How does it apply to your life?

WHAT WILL YOU DO?

How will you put this verse into practice?

NOW YOU PRAY

This is where you turn your thoughts into prayer. It could be a prayer of gratitude or praise. It could be a prayer of confession or a request for God's help. It's up to you. But take a minute to write a prayer of response to God.

MERCY FORGIVES THE FALLEN

Read this Scripture passage several times, slowly. Emphasize a different word or phrase each time you read the passage. Underline keywords or phrases that are especially meaningful to you. Then take a few minutes to write your thoughts on the journal page. Finish with a prayer.

"Then the master called the servant in. 'You wicked servant,' he said, 'I canceled all that debt of yours because you begged me to. Shouldn't you have had mercy on your fellow servant just as I had on you?' In anger his master turned him over to the jailers to be tortured, until he should pay back all he owed."

MATTHEW 18:32–34 (NIV)

WHAT DID YOU HEAR?

What did God say to you as you read today's Bible passage? What word or phrase was most meaningful to you?

WHAT DO YOU THINK?

What does this passage mean to you? How does it apply to your life?

WHAT WILL YOU DO?

How will you put this verse into practice?

NOW YOU PRAY

This is where you turn your thoughts into prayer. It could be a prayer of gratitude or praise. It could be a prayer of confession or a request for God's help. It's up to you. But take a minute to write a prayer of response to God.

MERCY FORGIVES THE FALLEN

Read this Scripture passage several times, slowly. Emphasize a different word or phrase each time you read the passage. Underline key words or phrases that are especially meaningful to you. Then take a few minutes to write your thoughts on the journal page. Finish with a prayer.

Never avenge yourselves. Leave that to God, for he has said that he will repay those who deserve it.

ROMANS 12:19 (TLB)

WHAT DID YOU HEAR?

What did God say to you as you read today's Bible passage? What word or phrase was most meaningful to you?

WHAT DO YOU THINK?

What does this passage mean to you? How does it apply to your life?

WHAT WILL YOU DO?

How will you put this verse into practice?

NOW YOU PRAY

This is where you turn your thoughts into prayer. It could be a prayer of gratitude or praise. It could be a prayer of confession or a request for God's help. It's up to you. But take a minute to write a prayer of response to God.

MERCY FORGIVES THE FALLEN

Read this Scripture passage several times, slowly. Emphasize a different word or phrase each time you read the passage. Underline keywords or phrases that are especially meaningful to you. Then take a few minutes to write your thoughts on the journal page. Finish with a prayer.

Be careful that none of you fails to respond to the grace which God gives, for if he does there can very easily spring up in him a bitter spirit which is not only bad in itself but can also poison the lives of many others.

HEBREWS 12:15 (PH)

WHAT DID YOU HEAR?

What did God say to you as you read today's Bible passage? What word or phrase was most meaningful to you?

WHAT DO YOU THINK?

What does this passage mean to you? How does it apply to your life?

WHAT WILL YOU DO?

How will you put this verse into practice?

NOW YOU PRAY

This is where you turn your thoughts into prayer. It could be a prayer of gratitude or praise. It could be a prayer of confession or a request for God's help. It's up to you. But take a minute to write a prayer of response to God.

MERCY FORGIVES THE FALLEN

Read this Scripture passage several times, slowly. Emphasize a different word or phrase each time you read the passage. Underline keywords or phrases that are especially meaningful to you. Then take a few minutes to write your thoughts on the journal page. Finish with a prayer.

We know that our old life died with Christ on the cross so that our sinful selves would have no power over us and we would not be slaves to sin.

ROMANS 6:6 (NCV)

WHAT DID YOU HEAR?

What did God say to you as you read today's Bible passage? What word or phrase was most meaningful to you?

WHAT DO YOU THINK?

What does this passage mean to you? How does it apply to your life?

WHAT WILL YOU DO?

How will you put this verse into practice?

NOW YOU PRAY

This is where you turn your thoughts into prayer. It could be a prayer of gratitude or praise. It could be a prayer of confession or a request for God's help. It's up to you. But take a minute to write a prayer of response to God.

MERCY HELPS THE HURTING

CHECKING IN

Choose one of these ideas to start your session.

- Share a verse that was especially meaningful to you in your *Miracle of Mercy Daily Devotions* this past week.

- Mercy is love in action. Did you witness an act of mercy this past week? If so, share your experience with the group.

MEMORY VERSE

Your own soul is nourished when you are kind.

PROVERBS 11:17 (TLB)

 ## WATCH THE VIDEO LESSON NOW AND FOLLOW ALONG IN YOUR OUTLINE.

MERCY HELPS THE HURTING

THREE RESPONSES TO PEOPLE IN NEED

- I keep my _____.

  "There was once a man who was going down from Jerusalem to Jericho when robbers attacked him, stripped him, and beat him up, leaving him half dead. It so happened that a priest was going down that road; but when he saw the man, he walked on by on the other side."

  LUKE 10:30–31 (TEV)

- I'm curious but _____.

  "In the same way a Levite also came there, went over and looked at the man, and then walked on by on the other side."

  LUKE 10:32 (TEV)

- I get close enough to _____.

  "But a Samaritan who was traveling that way came upon the man, and when he saw him, his heart was filled with pity. He went over to him, poured oil and wine on his wounds and bandaged them; then he put the man on his own animal and took him to an inn, where he took care of him. The next day he took out two silver coins and gave them to the innkeeper. 'Take care of him,' he told the innkeeper, 'and when I come back this way, I will pay you whatever else you spend on him.'" And Jesus concluded, "In your opinion, which one of these three acted like a neighbor toward the man attacked by the robbers?" The teacher of the Law answered, "The one who was kind to him." Jesus replied, "You go, then, and do the same."

  LUKE 10:33–37 (TEV)

Mercy takes action where others take off. Mercy isn't afraid to get its hands dirty. Mercy is about helping people, no matter who they are, what they look like, or where they come from. Serving others and following Christ go hand in hand.

FOUR STEPS TO SHOWING MERCY

- I must _____ of people around me.

Mercy always begins in the eyes. You have to see the need before you can meet the need.

> *"When* [the Samaritan] *saw the man, he felt compassion for him."*
>
> LUKE 10:33 (NLT[2005])

> *Do not look out only for yourselves. Look out for the good of others also.*
>
> 1 CORINTHIANS 10:24 (NCV)

- I must _____ with people's pain.

You see pain with your eyes, but you sympathize with your ears. Sometimes the greatest way to serve someone is just by listening.

> *Stoop down and reach out to those who are oppressed. Share their burdens, and so complete Christ's law.*
>
> GALATIANS 6:2 (MSG)

He comforts us in all our troubles so that we can comfort others. When they are troubled, we will be able to give them the same comfort God has given us.

2 CORINTHIANS 1:4 (NLT²⁰⁰⁵)

Be merciful to those who doubt.

JUDE 1:22 (NIV)

- **I must** _____ **and meet the need.**

Never walk away from someone who deserves help; your hand is God's hand for that person. Don't tell your neighbor, "Maybe some other time" or, "Try me tomorrow," when the money's right there in your pocket.

PROVERBS 3:27–28 (MSG)

"It so happened that a priest was going down that road."

LUKE 10:31 (TEV)

Ministry opportunities are usually unexpected. In order to seize the moment, you must be willing to be interrupted. What often seems like a coincidence in your life is really a God-engineered encounter. If you wait too long to respond, you might miss the moment.

Mercy touches the untouchable and loves the unlovable.

- **I must** _____ **whatever it takes.**

There is always a cost to kindness. There is always a sacrifice in service.

If you feed those who are hungry and take care of the needs of those who are troubled, then your light will shine in the darkness, and you will be bright like sunshine at noon. The Lord will always lead you. He will satisfy your needs in dry lands and give strength to your bones. You will be like a garden that has much water, like a spring that never runs dry.

ISAIAH 58:10–11 (NCV)

Your own soul is nourished when you are kind.

PROVERBS 11:17 (TLB)

"Blessed are the merciful, for they shall receive mercy."

MATTHEW 5:7 (ESV)

Faith that does nothing is worth nothing.

JAMES 2:20B (NCV)

DISCOVERY QUESTIONS

- Share a time in your life when other believers brought you comfort or met a need.

- Today's memory verse says, *"Your own soul is nourished when you are kind"* (Proverbs 11:17 TLB). Share a time when you found that to be true in your life.

- What can you do with what you've been through? The Bible says, "[God] *comforts us in all our troubles so that we can comfort others"* (2 Corinthians 1:4 NLT[2005]). What comfort has God given you when you were going through troubles? How can you share that comfort with others who are hurting?

- The Good Samaritan teaches us that ministry opportunities are usually unexpected, so we must be willing to be interrupted. Think of a time when God engineered an unexpected ministry opportunity just for you. How did you know it was God-engineered?

PUTTING IT INTO PRACTICE

PERSONAL

Pastor Rick said, "Mercy always begins in the eyes. You have to see the need before you can meet the need." To be a Good Samaritan, you must be willing to help people, no matter who they are, what they look like, or where they come from. It could be someone in your neighborhood, at work, or at school. It could be a shut-in, a loner, an immigrant, or a homeless person. Who needs you to be their "neighbor" like the Good Samaritan? What will you do to serve them this week?

- If you haven't already done so, decide which Mercy Project your group will complete. Visit *saddleback.com/mercyprojects* for a list of service ideas offered by each of our Saddleback campuses. Be sure to give yourselves a deadline for action. Without a date, it's not a plan, it's just an idea.

- Before your next meeting, your group's Mercy Project champion should go to *saddleback.com/mercyprojects* to sign up your group to serve.

DIVING DEEPER

Miracle of Mercy Daily Devotions. On pages 66–79, you will find Bible verses about helping the hurting, along with prompts for journaling your thoughts. Make the commitment with your group that you will give at least five minutes every day this week to read and meditate on these verses. Follow the prompts and write down your responses.

PRAYER DIRECTION

- Break into subgroups of two or three. Pray for the people you identified in the *Putting It into Practice* personal exercise. Ask God to give you the opportunity, courage, and grace to reach out to them this week.

- Pray that God will use your group to show the love of Christ to others through your Mercy Project.

- Share your prayer requests with your group and pray for each other. Be sure to record your prayer requests on the *Small Group Prayer* and *Praise Report* on page 156 of your study guide.

MERCY HELPS THE HURTING

Read this Scripture passage several times, slowly. Emphasize a different word or phrase each time you read the passage. Underline key words or phrases that are especially meaningful to you. Then take a few minutes to write your thoughts on the journal page. Finish with a prayer.

Your own soul is nourished when you are kind.

PROVERBS 11:17 (TLB)

WHAT DID YOU HEAR?

What did God say to you as you read today's Bible passage? What word or phrase was most meaningful to you?

WHAT DO YOU THINK?

What does this passage mean to you? How does it apply to your life?

WHAT WILL YOU DO?

How will you put this verse into practice?

NOW YOU PRAY

This is where you turn your thoughts into prayer. It could be a prayer of gratitude or praise. It could be a prayer of confession or a request for God's help. It's up to you. But take a minute to write a prayer of response to God.

MERCY HELPS THE HURTING

Read this Scripture passage several times, slowly. Emphasize a different word or phrase each time you read the passage. Underline keywords or phrases that are especially meaningful to you. Then take a few minutes to write your thoughts on the journal page. Finish with a prayer.

Do not look out only for yourselves. Look out for the good of others also.

1 CORINTHIANS 10:24 (NCV)

WHAT DID YOU HEAR?

What did God say to you as you read today's Bible passage? What word or phrase was most meaningful to you?

WHAT DO YOU THINK?

What does this passage mean to you? How does it apply to your life?

WHAT WILL YOU DO?

How will you put this verse into practice?

NOW YOU PRAY

This is where you turn your thoughts into prayer. It could be a prayer of gratitude or praise. It could be a prayer of confession or a request for God's help. It's up to you. But take a minute to write a prayer of response to God.

MERCY HELPS THE HURTING

Read this Scripture passage several times, slowly. Emphasize a different word or phrase each time you read the passage. Underline keywords or phrases that are especially meaningful to you. Then take a few minutes to write your thoughts on the journal page. Finish with a prayer.

Stoop down and reach out to those who are oppressed. Share their burdens, and so complete Christ's law.

GALATIANS 6:2 (MSG)

WHAT DID YOU HEAR?

What did God say to you as you read today's Bible passage? What word or phrase was most meaningful to you?

WHAT DO YOU THINK?

What does this passage mean to you? How does it apply to your life?

WHAT WILL YOU DO?

How will you put this verse into practice?

NOW YOU PRAY

This is where you turn your thoughts into prayer. It could be a prayer of gratitude or praise. It could be a prayer of confession or a request for God's help. It's up to you. But take a minute to write a prayer of response to God.

MERCY HELPS THE HURTING

Read this Scripture passage several times, slowly. Emphasize a different word or phrase each time you read the passage. Underline keywords or phrases that are especially meaningful to you. Then take a few minutes to write your thoughts on the journal page. Finish with a prayer.

He comforts us in all our troubles so that we can comfort others. When they are troubled, we will be able to give them the same comfort God has given us.

2 CORINTHIANS 1:4 (NLT[2005])

WHAT DID YOU HEAR?

What did God say to you as you read today's Bible passage? What word or phrase was most meaningful to you?

WHAT DO YOU THINK?

What does this passage mean to you? How does it apply to your life?

WHAT WILL YOU DO?

How will you put this verse into practice?

NOW YOU PRAY

This is where you turn your thoughts into prayer. It could be a prayer of gratitude or praise. It could be a prayer of confession or a request for God's help. It's up to you. But take a minute to write a prayer of response to God.

MERCY HELPS THE HURTING

Read this Scripture passage several times, slowly. Emphasize a different word or phrase each time you read the passage. Underline keywords or phrases that are especially meaningful to you. Then take a few minutes to write your thoughts on the journal page. Finish with a prayer.

Be merciful to those who doubt.

JUDE 1:22 (NIV)

WHAT DID YOU HEAR?

What did God say to you as you read today's Bible passage? What word or phrase was most meaningful to you?

WHAT DO YOU THINK?

What does this passage mean to you? How does it apply to your life?

WHAT WILL YOU DO?

How will you put this verse into practice?

NOW YOU PRAY

This is where you turn your thoughts into prayer. It could be a prayer of gratitude or praise. It could be a prayer of confession or a request for God's help. It's up to you. But take a minute to write a prayer of response to God.

MERCY HELPS THE HURTING

Read this Scripture passage several times, slowly. Emphasize a different word or phrase each time you read the passage. Underline keywords or phrases that are especially meaningful to you. Then take a few minutes to write your thoughts on the journal page. Finish with a prayer.

Never walk away from someone who deserves help; your hand is God's hand for that person. Don't tell your neighbor, "Maybe some other time" or, "Try me tomorrow," when the money's right there in your pocket.

PROVERBS 3:27-28 (MSG)

WHAT DID YOU HEAR?

What did God say to you as you read today's Bible passage? What word or phrase was most meaningful to you?

WHAT DO YOU THINK?

What does this passage mean to you? How does it apply to your life?

WHAT WILL YOU DO?

How will you put this verse into practice?

NOW YOU PRAY

This is where you turn your thoughts into prayer. It could be a prayer of gratitude or praise. It could be a prayer of confession or a request for God's help. It's up to you. But take a minute to write a prayer of response to God.

MERCY HELPS THE HURTING

Read this Scripture passage several times, slowly. Emphasize a different word or phrase each time you read the passage. Underline keywords or phrases that are especially meaningful to you. Then take a few minutes to write your thoughts on the journal page. Finish with a prayer.

Faith that does nothing is worth nothing.

JAMES 2:20b (NCV)

WHAT DID YOU HEAR?

What did God say to you as you read today's Bible passage? What word or phrase was most meaningful to you?

WHAT DO YOU THINK?

What does this passage mean to you? How does it apply to your life?

WHAT WILL YOU DO?

How will you put this verse into practice?

NOW YOU PRAY

This is where you turn your thoughts into prayer. It could be a prayer of gratitude or praise. It could be a prayer of confession or a request for God's help. It's up to you. But take a minute to write a prayer of response to God.

MERCY IS PATIENT WITH DIFFICULT PEOPLE

SESSION FOUR

CHECKING IN

Choose one of these ideas to start your session.

- Share a verse that was especially meaningful to you in your *Miracle of Mercy Daily Devotions* this past week.

- What did God reveal to you through your personal *Putting It into Practice* effort last week? How was your soul nourished by offering kindness to others?

MEMORY VERSE

Mercy triumphs over judgment.

JAMES 2:13b (NIV)

WATCH THE VIDEO LESSON NOW AND FOLLOW ALONG IN YOUR OUTLINE.

MERCY IS PATIENT WITH DIFFICULT PEOPLE

• _____ •

Hurt people hurt people. You must look past their behavior and see their pain.

> *When a fool is annoyed, he quickly lets it be known. Smart people will ignore an insult.*
>
> **PROVERBS 12:16 (TEV)**

• _____ •

Your emotional and spiritual maturity is largely measured by how you treat people who mistreat you.

When you give up control of your emotions, you lose control of your tongue.

> *Watch your words and hold your tongue; you'll save yourself a lot of grief.*
>
> **PROVERBS 21:23 (MSG)**

> *It is better to be patient than powerful; it is better to have self-control than to conquer a city.*
>
> **PROVERBS 16:32 (NLT)**

Learn to pray, "God, give me a tender heart and a tough hide."

> *A man's wisdom gives him patience; it is to his glory to overlook an offense.*
>
> **PROVERBS 19:11 (NIV)**

Be patient with each other, making allowance for each other's faults because of your love.

EPHESIANS 4:2b (TLB)

The man who makes no allowances for others will find none made for him.

JAMES 2:13a (PH)

"Blessed are the merciful for they will be shown mercy."

MATTHEW 5:7 (NIV)

You must make allowance for each other's faults and forgive the person who offends you. Remember, the Lord forgave you, so you must forgive others.

COLOSSIANS 3:13 (NLT)

Disregarding another person's faults preserves love; [gossiping] *about them separates close friends.*

PROVERBS 17:9 (NLT)

Without wood a fire goes out; without gossip a quarrel dies down.

PROVERBS 26:20 (NIV)

Gossip just adds fuel to the fire. It perpetuates the pain.

*Whatever is true, whatever is noble, whatever is right,
whatever is pure, whatever is lovely, whatever is admirable—
if anything is excellent or praiseworthy—think about such
things . . . And the God of peace will be with you.*

PHILIPPIANS 4:8–9 (NIV)

If you want peace in your life, then let go of the offense, refuse to gossip about it, and focus on the goodness of God.

- _____ .

*Just as charcoal and wood keep a fire going, a quarrelsome
person keeps an argument going.*

PROVERBS 26:21 (NCV)

Sometimes the most merciful thing you can do is walk away from an argument.

- _____ .

Mercy triumphs over judgment.

JAMES 2:13b (NIV)

Do not repay . . . insult with insult.

1 PETER 3:9 (NIV)

*Clothe yourselves with tenderhearted mercy, kindness,
humility, gentleness, and patience . . . Above all, clothe
yourselves with love, which binds us all together in
perfect harmony.*

COLOSSIANS 3:12b, 14 (NLT²⁰⁰⁵)

*Ask God to bless those who persecute you—yes, ask him to
bless, not to curse.*

ROMANS 12:14 (TEV)

*If someone has done you wrong, do not repay him with
a wrong. Try to do what everyone considers to be good.*

Do everything possible on your part to live in peace with everybody.

ROMANS 12:17–18 (TEV)

Do not let evil defeat you; instead, conquer evil with good.

ROMANS 12:21 (TEV)

If your group is coed, we recommend that you break into subgroups by gender to encourage openness in your discussion. This will be especially helpful in the *Putting It into Practice* and *Prayer Direction* sections of your study.

DISCOVERY QUESTIONS

- Pastor Rick identified six practices for dealing with difficult people in your life. In which of these practices does God seem to be giving you the greatest "opportunity" to grow right now?

- Today's memory verse says, *"Mercy triumphs over judgment"* (James 2:13b NIV). Why is mercy so important to God?

- The Bible says, *"Clothe yourselves with tenderhearted mercy, kindness, humility, gentleness, and patience . . . Above all, clothe yourselves with love, which binds us all together in perfect harmony"* (Colossians 3:12b, 14 NLT[2005]). What does it mean to "clothe yourself" with those things, and how can you do it?

- The Bible says, *"Ask God to bless those who persecute you—yes, ask him to bless, not to curse"* (Romans 12:14 TEV). How will you respond if God answers that prayer by blessing your enemy?

PUTTING IT INTO PRACTICE

PERSONAL

God hates gossip. In Romans 1:29, he puts gossip in the same list of sins as murder, sexual immorality, and violence. So make the commitment to your group that if someone irritates you this week, and you just *have* to gossip about it, that you will only "gossip" with God! That's called prayer! Tell God—and only God—all about it, and then leave it in his hands. Sign your name on the signature line below.

> *If I am hurt, shocked, scandalized, irritated, disappointed, or otherwise offended with anyone this week, I hereby promise that I will talk only with God and with no one else.*

_____

(Me)

- If you haven't already done so, complete your plans for your group's Mercy Project. Discuss the "who, what, when, where, and how" details of your project, and divide up the responsibilities. If you still need serving opportunities or ideas, visit *saddleback .com/mercyprojects*.

- If you have completed your project, visit *saddleback.com/yourstory* and share your experience of how the Mercy Project impacted your group.

DIVING DEEPER

- *Miracle of Mercy Daily Devotions.* On pages 88–101, you will find Bible verses about getting along with difficult people, along with prompts for journaling your thoughts. Make the commitment with your group that you will give at least five minutes every day this week to read and meditate on these verses. Follow the prompts and write down your responses.

PRAYER DIRECTION

- Ask God to give you "a tender heart and a tough hide" so you can be patient with the difficult people in your life. Pray for wisdom to look behind their behavior and understand their pain.

- Pray for your group's Mercy Project.

- Share your prayer requests with your group and pray for each other. Be sure to record your prayer requests on the *Small Group Prayer* and *Praise Report* on page 156 of your study guide.

MERCY IS PATIENT WITH DIFFICULT PEOPLE

Read this Scripture passage several times, slowly. Emphasize a different word or phrase each time you read the passage. Underline keywords or phrases that are especially meaningful to you. Then take a few minutes to write your thoughts on the journal page. Finish with a prayer.

Mercy triumphs over judgment.

JAMES 2:13b (NIV)

WHAT DID YOU HEAR?

What did God say to you as you read today's Bible passage? What word or phrase was most meaningful to you?

WHAT DO YOU THINK?

What does this passage mean to you? How does it apply to your life?

WHAT WILL YOU DO?

How will you put this verse into practice?

NOW YOU PRAY

This is where you turn your thoughts into prayer. It could be a prayer of gratitude or praise. It could be a prayer of confession or a request for God's help. It's up to you. But take a minute to write a prayer of response to God.

MERCY IS PATIENT WITH DIFFICULT PEOPLE

Read this Scripture passage several times, slowly. Emphasize a different word or phrase each time you read the passage. Underline key words or phrases that are especially meaningful to you. Then take a few minutes to write your thoughts on the journal page. Finish with a prayer.

Watch your words and hold your tongue; you'll save yourself a lot of grief.

PROVERBS 21:23 (MSG)

WHAT DID YOU HEAR?

What did God say to you as you read today's Bible passage? What word or phrase was most meaningful to you?

WHAT DO YOU THINK?

What does this passage mean to you? How does it apply to your life?

WHAT WILL YOU DO?

How will you put this verse into practice?

NOW YOU PRAY

This is where you turn your thoughts into prayer. It could be a prayer of gratitude or praise. It could be a prayer of confession or a request for God's help. It's up to you. But take a minute to write a prayer of response to God.

MERCY IS PATIENT WITH DIFFICULT PEOPLE

Read this Scripture passage several times, slowly. Emphasize a different word or phrase each time you read the passage. Underline keywords or phrases that are especially meaningful to you. Then take a few minutes to write your thoughts on the journal page. Finish with a prayer.

It is better to be patient than powerful; it is better to have self-control than to conquer a city.

PROVERBS 16:32 (NLT)

WHAT DID YOU HEAR?

What did God say to you as you read today's Bible passage? What word or phrase was most meaningful to you?

WHAT DO YOU THINK?

What does this passage mean to you? How does it apply to your life?

WHAT WILL YOU DO?

How will you put this verse into practice?

NOW YOU PRAY

This is where you turn your thoughts into prayer. It could be a prayer of gratitude or praise. It could be a prayer of confession or a request for God's help. It's up to you. But take a minute to write a prayer of response to God.

MERCY IS PATIENT WITH DIFFICULT PEOPLE

Read this Scripture passage several times, slowly. Emphasize a different word or phrase each time you read the passage. Underline keywords or phrases that are especially meaningful to you. Then take a few minutes to write your thoughts on the journal page. Finish with a prayer.

You must make allowance for each other's faults and forgive the person who offends you. Remember, the Lord forgave you, so you must forgive others.

COLOSSIANS 3:13 (NLT)

WHAT DID YOU HEAR?

What did God say to you as you read today's Bible passage? What word or phrase was most meaningful to you?

WHAT DO YOU THINK?

What does this passage mean to you? How does it apply to your life?

WHAT WILL YOU DO?

How will you put this verse into practice?

NOW YOU PRAY

This is where you turn your thoughts into prayer. It could be a prayer of gratitude or praise. It could be a prayer of confession or a request for God's help. It's up to you. But take a minute to write a prayer of response to God.

MERCY IS PATIENT WITH DIFFICULT PEOPLE

Read this Scripture passage several times, slowly. Emphasize a different word or phrase each time you read the passage. Underline keywords or phrases that are especially meaningful to you. Then take a few minutes to write your thoughts on the journal page. Finish with a prayer.

Whatever is true, whatever is noble, whatever is right, whatever is pure, whatever is lovely, whatever is admirable—if anything is excellent or praiseworthy—think about such things . . . And the God of peace will be with you.

PHILIPPIANS 4:8–9 (NIV)

WHAT DID YOU HEAR?

What did God say to you as you read today's Bible passage? What word or phrase was most meaningful to you?

WHAT DO YOU THINK?

What does this passage mean to you? How does it apply to your life?

WHAT WILL YOU DO?

How will you put this verse into practice?

NOW YOU PRAY

This is where you turn your thoughts into prayer. It could be a prayer of gratitude or praise. It could be a prayer of confession or a request for God's help. It's up to you. But take a minute to write a prayer of response to God.

MERCY IS PATIENT WITH DIFFICULT PEOPLE

Read this Scripture passage several times, slowly. Emphasize a different word or phrase each time you read the passage. Underline key words or phrases that are especially meaningful to you. Then take a few minutes to write your thoughts on the journal page. Finish with a prayer.

Clothe yourselves with tenderhearted mercy, kindness, humility, gentleness, and patience . . . Above all, clothe yourselves with love, which binds us all together in perfect harmony.

COLOSSIANS 3:12b, 14 (NLT[2005])

WHAT DID YOU HEAR?

What did God say to you as you read today's Bible passage? What word or phrase was most meaningful to you?

WHAT DO YOU THINK?

What does this passage mean to you? How does it apply to your life?

WHAT WILL YOU DO?

How will you put this verse into practice?

NOW YOU PRAY

This is where you turn your thoughts into prayer. It could be a prayer of gratitude or praise. It could be a prayer of confession or a request for God's help. It's up to you. But take a minute to write a prayer of response to God.

MERCY IS PATIENT WITH DIFFICULT PEOPLE

Read this Scripture passage several times, slowly. Emphasize a different word or phrase each time you read the passage. Underline keywords or phrases that are especially meaningful to you. Then take a few minutes to write your thoughts on the journal page. Finish with a prayer.

Ask God to bless those who persecute you—yes, ask him to bless, not to curse.

ROMANS 12:14 (TEV)

WHAT DID YOU HEAR?

What did God say to you as you read today's Bible passage? What word or phrase was most meaningful to you?

WHAT DO YOU THINK?

What does this passage mean to you? How does it apply to your life?

WHAT WILL YOU DO?

How will you put this verse into practice?

NOW YOU PRAY

This is where you turn your thoughts into prayer. It could be a prayer of gratitude or praise. It could be a prayer of confession or a request for God's help. It's up to you. But take a minute to write a prayer of response to God.

MERCY IS KIND TO ENEMIES

CHECKING IN

Choose one of these ideas to start your session.

- Share a verse that was especially meaningful to you in your *Miracle of Mercy Daily Devotions* this past week.

- How did you do with the "no gossip" covenant you signed in your personal *Putting It into Practice* exercise last week?

MEMORY VERSE

Be quick to listen, slow to speak and slow to become angry.

JAMES 1:19b (NIV)

WATCH THE VIDEO LESSON NOW AND FOLLOW ALONG IN YOUR OUTLINE.

MERCY IS KIND TO ENEMIES

The best way to eliminate an enemy is to turn him into a friend; and the best way to do that is to treat him with kindness.

"Love your enemies, do good to those who hate you."

LUKE 6:27 (NIV)

Peacekeepers avoid conflict and pretend it doesn't exist. Peacemakers, on the other hand, resolve conflict and reconcile relationships.

"Blessed are the peacemakers: for they shall be called the children of God."

MATTHEW 5:9 (KJV)

Those who are peacemakers will plant seeds of peace and reap a harvest of goodness.

JAMES 3:18 (TLB)

SEVEN STEPS OF RECONCILIATION

1. _____.

"If you are about to place your gift on the altar and remember that someone is angry with you, leave your gift there in front of the altar. Make peace with that person, then come back and offer your gift to God."

MATTHEW 5:23-24 (CEV)

It's more important to be reconciled than religious.

While we were still sinners, Christ died for us . . . While we were enemies we were reconciled to God by the death of his Son.

ROMANS 5:8-10 (ESV)

If your enemy is hungry, feed him; if he is thirsty, give him something to drink ... Do not be overcome by evil, but overcome evil with good.

ROMANS 12:20–21 (NIV)

- The only way to resolve a conflict is to _____ .

2. _____ .

If you want to know what God wants you to do, ask him, and he will gladly tell you.

JAMES 1:5 (TLB)

The right word at the right time is like precious gold set in silver.

PROVERBS 25:11 (CEV)

3. _____ .

Pride only leads to arguments.

PROVERBS 13:10 (NCV)

What causes fights and quarrels among you? Aren't they caused by the selfish desires that fight to control you?

JAMES 4:1 (GW)

"Why, then, do you look at the speck in your brother's eye and pay no attention to the log in your own eye? ... First take the log out of your own eye, and then you will be able to see clearly to take the speck out of your brother's eye."

MATTHEW 7:3–5 (TEV)

4. _____.

The people who need love the most are those who deserve it the least.

> *Be quick to listen, slow to speak and slow to become angry.*
> **JAMES 1:19b (NIV)**

God gave you two ears and one mouth. That means you should always listen twice as much as you speak.

> *Each of you should look not only to your own interests, but also to the interests of others. Your attitude should be the same as that of Christ Jesus.*
> **PHILIPPIANS 2:4–5 (NIV)**

5. _____.

> *Speak the truth in love.*
> **EPHESIANS 4:15 (NLT²⁰⁰⁵)**

The truth is not enough. It's not just what you say, but how you say it. If you speak offensively, it will be received defensively. You are never persuasive when you are abrasive. You never get your point across by being cross.

> *You must no longer say insulting or cruel things about others.*
> **COLOSSIANS 3:8b (CEV)**

> *Do not use harmful words, but only helpful words, the kind that build up and provide what is needed, so that what you say will do good to those who hear you.*
> **EPHESIANS 4:29 (TEV)**

> *Reckless words pierce like a sword, but the tongue of the wise brings healing.*
> **PROVERBS 12:18 (NIV)**

6. _____.

The blame game is a waste of time. As long as you're fixing the blame, you are not fixing the problem. As long as you're attacking each other, you're not attacking the issues.

7. _____ .

There are some things we'll never agree on because we're all different. But you can disagree without being disagreeable. You can have unity without uniformity. You can walk hand in hand without seeing eye to eye. You can have reconciliation without resolution.

> *God has not given us a spirit of fear and timidity, but of*
> *power, love, and self-discipline.*
>
> 2 TIMOTHY 1:7 (NLT)

If your group is coed, we recommend that you break into subgroups by gender to encourage openness in your discussion. This will be especially helpful in the *Putting It into Practice* and *Prayer Direction* sections of your study.

DISCOVERY QUESTIONS

- Some people hate conflict and do all they can to avoid it; others face it head-on. What is your typical response to conflict?

- The Bible says, *"Those who are peacemakers will plant seeds of peace and reap a harvest of goodness"* (James 3:18 TLB). In what relationship do you need to plant a seed of peace? What would that look like for you?

- Which of the seven steps of reconciliation is most challenging for you?

- Pastor Rick said, "You can disagree without being disagreeable. You can have unity without uniformity. You can walk hand in hand without seeing eye to eye." Talk about the difference between reconciliation and resolution. How can you have one without the other?

PUTTING IT INTO PRACTICE

PERSONAL

Is it time for you to plan a peace conference to reconcile a broken relationship? What's one thing you will do this week to begin the peace process?

GROUP

Share your experience! If you have completed your Mercy Project, tell us how God used your group to show Christ's love and mercy to others. Visit *saddleback.com/yourstory* and share what God has done.

DIVING DEEPER

Miracle of Mercy Daily Devotions. On pages 112–125, you will find Bible verses about reconciling broken relationships, along with prompts for journaling your thoughts. Make the commitment with your group that you will give at least five minutes every day this week to read and meditate on these verses. Follow the prompts and write down your responses.

PRAYER DIRECTION

If you haven't already done so, we recommend that you break into subgroups by gender for your prayer time in this session. It will give you the opportunity to go deeper in your sharing.

- Do you need to reconcile a relationship? You don't have to go into specific details, but join with two or three members of your group and ask them to pray with you right now. Pray first of all that God will prepare your heart and show you where you have been wrong in the relationship. Ask God to give you direction and the right timing to initiate the conversation. Ask God to give you favor with that person, and to give you the ability, wisdom, and courage to speak—and listen—with gentleness, honesty, and genuine love.

- Share your prayer requests with your group and pray for each other. Be sure to record your prayer requests on the *Small Group Prayer* and *Praise Report* on page 156 of your study guide.

BEFORE YOU GO

There is just one session left in this study. Take a few minutes to talk about what your group will study next. We invite you to visit our *Daily Hope* website at *rickwarren.org*, where you can find more video-based small group studies. You can also sign up to receive *Daily Hope*, Pastor Rick's free daily devotional email.

Start making plans for an evening meal or a picnic with your group to celebrate what God has done in your lives through this study of *The Miracle of Mercy*. A party is an excellent opportunity for you to invite new people who might be interested in joining your group. Talk about your celebration before you leave your meeting. Where will you have your party? When will you have it? Will it be a potluck, will someone barbecue, or will you call out for pizza? Divide up the responsibilities, and then get ready to enjoy a great time of fellowship together.

MYSADDLEBACK.COM
We invite all our faithful Saddleback small groups to visit *mysaddleback.com* and explore all the FREE small group curriculum choices for your group.

MERCY IS KIND TO ENEMIES

Read this Scripture passage several times, slowly. Emphasize a different word or phrase each time you read the passage. Underline keywords or phrases that are especially meaningful to you. Then take a few minutes to write your thoughts on the journal page. Finish with a prayer.

Be quick to listen, slow to speak and slow to become angry.

JAMES 1:19b (NIV)

WHAT DID YOU HEAR?

What did God say to you as you read today's Bible passage? What word or phrase was most meaningful to you?

WHAT DO YOU THINK?

What does this passage mean to you? How does it apply to your life?

WHAT WILL YOU DO?

How will you put this verse into practice?

NOW YOU PRAY

This is where you turn your thoughts into prayer. It could be a prayer of gratitude or praise. It could be a prayer of confession or a request for God's help. It's up to you. But take a minute to write a prayer of response to God.

MERCY IS KIND TO ENEMIES

Read this Scripture passage several times, slowly. Emphasize a different word or phrase each time you read the passage. Underline keywords or phrases that are especially meaningful to you. Then take a few minutes to write your thoughts on the journal page. Finish with a prayer.

Those who are peacemakers will plant seeds of peace and reap a harvest of goodness.

JAMES 3:18 (TLB)

WHAT DID YOU HEAR?

What did God say to you as you read today's Bible passage? What word or phrase was most meaningful to you?

WHAT DO YOU THINK?

What does this passage mean to you? How does it apply to your life?

WHAT WILL YOU DO?

How will you put this verse into practice?

NOW YOU PRAY

This is where you turn your thoughts into prayer. It could be a prayer of gratitude or praise. It could be a prayer of confession or a request for God's help. It's up to you. But take a minute to write a prayer of response to God.

MERCY IS KIND TO ENEMIES

Read this Scripture passage several times, slowly. Emphasize a different word or phrase each time you read the passage. Underline keywords or phrases that are especially meaningful to you. Then take a few minutes to write your thoughts on the journal page. Finish with a prayer.

If your enemy is hungry, feed him; if he is thirsty, give him something to drink … Do not be overcome by evil, but overcome evil with good.

ROMANS 12:20–21 (NIV)

WHAT DID YOU HEAR?

What did God say to you as you read today's Bible passage? What word or phrase was most meaningful to you?

WHAT DO YOU THINK?

What does this passage mean to you? How does it apply to your life?

WHAT WILL YOU DO?

How will you put this verse into practice?

NOW YOU PRAY

This is where you turn your thoughts into prayer. It could be a prayer of gratitude or praise. It could be a prayer of confession or a request for God's help. It's up to you. But take a minute to write a prayer of response to God.

MERCY IS KIND TO ENEMIES

Read this Scripture passage several times, slowly. Emphasize a different word or phrase each time you read the passage. Underline key words or phrases that are especially meaningful to you. Then take a few minutes to write your thoughts on the journal page. Finish with a prayer.

"Why, then, do you look at the speck in your brother's eye and pay no attention to the log in your own eye? … First take the log out of your own eye, and then you will be able to see clearly to take the speck out of your brother's eye."

MATTHEW 7:3–5 (TEV)

WHAT DID YOU HEAR?

What did God say to you as you read today's Bible passage? What word or phrase was most meaningful to you?

WHAT DO YOU THINK?

What does this passage mean to you? How does it apply to your life?

WHAT WILL YOU DO?

How will you put this verse into practice?

NOW YOU PRAY

This is where you turn your thoughts into prayer. It could be a prayer of gratitude or praise. It could be a prayer of confession or a request for God's help. It's up to you. But take a minute to write a prayer of response to God.

MERCY IS KIND TO ENEMIES

Read this Scripture passage several times, slowly. Emphasize a different word or phrase each time you read the passage. Underline keywords or phrases that are especially meaningful to you. Then take a few minutes to write your thoughts on the journal page. Finish with a prayer.

Speak the truth in love.

EPHESIANS 4:15 (NLT[2005])

WHAT DID YOU HEAR?

What did God say to you as you read today's Bible passage? What word or phrase was most meaningful to you?

_____

_____

_____

_____

WHAT DO YOU THINK?

What does this passage mean to you? How does it apply to your life?

_____

_____

_____

_____

WHAT WILL YOU DO?

How will you put this verse into practice?

_____

_____

_____

_____

NOW YOU PRAY

This is where you turn your thoughts into prayer. It could be a prayer of gratitude or praise. It could be a prayer of confession or a request for God's help. It's up to you. But take a minute to write a prayer of response to God.

_____

_____

_____

_____

_____

MERCY IS KIND TO ENEMIES

Read this Scripture passage several times, slowly. Emphasize a different word or phrase each time you read the passage. Underline keywords or phrases that are especially meaningful to you. Then take a few minutes to write your thoughts on the journal page. Finish with a prayer.

Do not use harmful words, but only helpful words, the kind that build up and provide what is needed, so that what you say will do good to those who hear you.

EPHESIANS 4:29 (TEV)

WHAT DID YOU HEAR?

What did God say to you as you read today's Bible passage? What word or phrase was most meaningful to you?

WHAT DO YOU THINK?

What does this passage mean to you? How does it apply to your life?

WHAT WILL YOU DO?

How will you put this verse into practice?

NOW YOU PRAY

This is where you turn your thoughts into prayer. It could be a prayer of gratitude or praise. It could be a prayer of confession or a request for God's help. It's up to you. But take a minute to write a prayer of response to God.

MERCY IS KIND TO ENEMIES

Read this Scripture passage several times, slowly. Emphasize a different word or phrase each time you read the passage. Underline keywords or phrases that are especially meaningful to you. Then take a few minutes to write your thoughts on the journal page. Finish with a prayer.

God has not given us a spirit of fear and timidity, but of power, love, and self-discipline.

2 TIMOTHY 1:7 (NLT)

WHAT DID YOU HEAR?

What did God say to you as you read today's Bible passage? What word or phrase was most meaningful to you?

WHAT DO YOU THINK?

What does this passage mean to you? How does it apply to your life?

WHAT WILL YOU DO?

How will you put this verse into practice?

NOW YOU PRAY

This is where you turn your thoughts into prayer. It could be a prayer of gratitude or praise. It could be a prayer of confession or a request for God's help. It's up to you. But take a minute to write a prayer of response to God.

MERCY CARES FOR THE LOST

SESSION SIX

CHECKING IN

Choose one of these ideas to start your session.

- Share a verse that was especially meaningful to you in your *Miracle of Mercy Daily Devotions* this past week.

- In our previous session, you were encouraged to plant a seed of peace in a broken relationship. Would anyone like to share your experience with putting your plan into action?

MEMORY VERSE

Always be prepared to give an answer to everyone who asks you to give the reason for the hope that you have. But do this with gentleness and respect.

1 PETER 3:15b (NIV)

 WATCH THE VIDEO LESSON NOW AND FOLLOW ALONG IN YOUR OUTLINE.

MERCY CARES FOR THE LOST

Mercy does all it can to keep people from going to hell.

> *In the same way that you, [Father], gave me a mission in the world, I give them a mission in the world.*
>
> JOHN 17:18 (MSG)

> [God] *reconciled us to himself through Christ and gave us the ministry of reconciliation.*
>
> 2 CORINTHIANS 5:18b (NIV)

Is anybody going to be in heaven because of you? You don't have to be perfect, or spiritually mature, or a Bible scholar. All you have to know is that Jesus has made a difference in your life.

> *Always be prepared to give an answer to everyone who asks you to give the reason for the hope that you have. But do this with gentleness and respect.*
>
> 1 PETER 3:15b (NIV)

God doesn't expect you to fulfill your mission on your own. Evangelism is something you can do as a small group.

> *We work together as partners who belong to God.*
>
> 1 CORINTHIANS 3:9 (NLT)

> *One day as Jesus was teaching, Pharisees and religion teachers were sitting around . . . The healing power of God was on him. Some men arrived carrying a paraplegic on a stretcher. They were looking for a way to get into the house and set him before Jesus. When they couldn't find a way in because of the crowd, they went up on the roof, removed some tiles, and let him down in the middle of everyone, right in front of Jesus. Impressed by their bold belief, he said, "Friend, I forgive your sins." That set the religion scholars and Pharisees buzzing. "Who does he think he is? That's blasphemous talk. God and only God can forgive sins." Jesus knew exactly what they were thinking and*

said, "Why all this gossipy whispering? Which is simpler: to say 'I forgive your sins,' or to say 'Get up and start walking?' Well, just so it's clear that I'm the Son of Man and authorized to do either, or both . . ." He now spoke directly to the paraplegic: "Get up. Take your bedroll and go home." Without a moment's hesitation, he did it—got up, took his blanket, and left for home, giving glory to God all the way. The people rubbed their eyes, incredulous—and then also gave glory to God. Awestruck, they said, "We've never seen anything like that!"

LUKE 5:17–26 (MSG)

FIVE WAYS YOUR SMALL GROUP CAN CARE FOR THE LOST

- The Principle of _____.

Love opens the door for you to share Christ with others. People don't care how much you know until they know how much you care.

We should all be concerned about our neighbor and the good things that will build his faith.

ROMANS 15:2 (GW)

- The Principle of _____.

Sometimes it takes a team to win someone for Christ.

After all, who is Apollos? Who is Paul? We are only God's servants through whom you believed the Good News. Each of us did the work the Lord gave us. I planted the seed in your hearts, and Apollos watered it, but it was God who made it grow. It's not important who does the planting, or who does the watering. What's important is that God makes the seed grow. The one who plants and the one who waters work together with the same purpose. And both will be rewarded for their own hard work.

1 CORINTHIANS 3:5–8 (NLT[2005])

- **The Principle of** _____.

*When Jesus saw their faith, he said, "Friend, your sins
are forgiven."*

LUKE 5:20 (NIV)

*[Jesus] is able, now and always, to save those who come to
God through him.*

HEBREWS 7:25 (TEV)

- **The Principle of** _____.

*Be wise in the way you act toward outsiders; make the most
of every opportunity.*

COLOSSIANS 4:5 (NIV)

*"Go out into the country lanes and behind the hedges and
urge anyone you find to come, so that the house will be full."*

LUKE 14:23 (NLT)

Jesus says to the world, "Come and see;" but to us he says, "Go and tell."

- **The Principle of** _____.

*The Lord is . . . not willing that any should perish but that all
should come to repentance.*

2 PETER 3:9 (NKJV)

Helping someone get into heaven is the greatest act of mercy you can do
for them.

DISCOVERY QUESTIONS

- If you want to know God's plan for reaching the world for Jesus Christ, look around the room. You're it. You are God's plan, because God works through his people. Does that thought excite you, scare you, or overwhelm you?

- Read 1 Peter 3:15b aloud together—*"Always be prepared to give an answer to everyone who asks you to give the reason for the hope that you have. But do this with gentleness and respect."* Break the verse down phrase by phrase. What principles do you observe about sharing Christ with others?

- If somebody hadn't cared enough to tell you the Good News, you would be living without Christ right now. Who do you know that needs to hear about God's mercy in Jesus Christ? Write their name in the space below. During your closing prayer time, pray together for all of the names your group members have written down.

_____

(Name)

- What is the most important lesson you have learned in your study of *The Miracle of Mercy*?

PUTTING IT INTO PRACTICE

- Are you prepared to "give the reason for the hope that *you* have"? For the next ten minutes, pair up with one other person and practice telling your story by answering these three questions:

  › What was your life like before you knew Jesus Christ?

  › How did you meet him?

  › What difference has he made in your life?

- We would love to hear how God has changed your life through *The Miracle of Mercy* study. By sharing your story, you can inspire and encourage others. Have you experienced forgiveness, compassion for the hurting, reconciliation in a relationship, or a change of heart toward a particularly difficult person in your life? Go to *saddleback.com/yourstory* to tell us about your experience.

- By now you might have completed your Mercy Project, or you might still be in the planning stage. Wherever you are in the process, we want to challenge you to go one step further. Would you prayerfully consider making a one-year commitment to doing Mercy Projects as a group? As Pastor Rick said in Session One, "Mercy is more than an attitude. Mercy is a lifestyle." Our hope is that you will look back and not say, "Look at what we did," but rather say, "Look at what we started!" What can your group do to make Mercy Projects a part of the life of your group? Find more opportunities to serve at *saddleback.com/mercyprojects*.

DIVING DEEPER

The Miracle of Mercy Daily Devotions. On pages 136–145, you will find Bible verses about caring for lost people, along with prompts for journaling your thoughts. Make the commitment with your group that you will give at least five minutes every day this week to read and meditate on these verses. Follow the prompts and write down your responses.

PRAYER DIRECTION

- Pastor Rick asked each of you to come up with a name of someone who doesn't know Jesus and pray together for them. Here are three ways you can pray:

    › Ask God to soften your heart and give you his love for the people in your life who don't know Jesus Christ.

    › Ask God to give you opportunities and the courage to "give them the reason for the hope that you have," and to invite them to church or your small group.

    › Ask God to soften *their* hearts and prepare them to hear the Good News of Jesus Christ.

- Share your prayer requests with your group and pray for each other. Be sure to record your prayer requests on the *Small Group Prayer* and *Praise Report* on page 156 of your study guide.

BEFORE YOU GO

- Pastor Rick would love to hear your story of what this study has meant to you. You can write to him at *pastorrick@saddleback.com*.

- Visit our *Daily Hope* website at *rickwarren.org*, where you can find more video-based small group studies. You can also sign up to receive *Daily Hope*, Pastor Rick's free daily devotional email.

- Have you made plans for a party with your group to celebrate what God has done in your lives through this study of *The Miracle of Mercy*? A party is an excellent opportunity for you to invite new people who might be interested in joining your group. Talk about your celebration before you leave your meeting. Where will you have your party? When will you have it? Will it be a potluck, will someone barbecue, or will you call out for pizza? Divide up the responsibilities and get ready to enjoy a great time of fellowship together.

MYSADDLEBACK.COM

We invite all our faithful Saddleback small groups to visit *mysaddleback.com* and explore all the FREE small group curriculum choices for your group.

MERCY CARES FOR THE LOST

Read this Scripture passage several times, slowly. Emphasize a different word or phrase each time you read the passage. Underline keywords or phrases that are especially meaningful to you. Then take a few minutes to write your thoughts on the journal page. Finish with a prayer.

Always be prepared to give an answer to everyone who asks you to give the reason for the hope that you have. But do this with gentleness and respect.

1 PETER 3:15b (NIV)

WHAT DID YOU HEAR?

What did God say to you as you read today's Bible passage? What word or phrase was most meaningful to you?

WHAT DO YOU THINK?

What does this passage mean to you? How does it apply to your life?

WHAT WILL YOU DO?

How will you put this verse into practice?

NOW YOU PRAY

This is where you turn your thoughts into prayer. It could be a prayer of gratitude or praise. It could be a prayer of confession or a request for God's help. It's up to you. But take a minute to write a prayer of response to God.

MERCY CARES FOR THE LOST

Read this Scripture passage several times, slowly. Emphasize a different word or phrase each time you read the passage. Underline keywords or phrases that are especially meaningful to you. Then take a few minutes to write your thoughts on the journal page. Finish with a prayer.

[God] reconciled us to himself through Christ and gave us the ministry of reconciliation.

2 CORINTHIANS 5:18b (NIV)

WHAT DID YOU HEAR?

What did God say to you as you read today's Bible passage? What word or phrase was most meaningful to you?

_____

_____

_____

_____

WHAT DO YOU THINK?

What does this passage mean to you? How does it apply to your life?

_____

_____

_____

_____

WHAT WILL YOU DO?

How will you put this verse into practice?

_____

_____

_____

_____

NOW YOU PRAY

This is where you turn your thoughts into prayer. It could be a prayer of gratitude or praise. It could be a prayer of confession or a request for God's help. It's up to you. But take a minute to write a prayer of response to God.

_____

_____

_____

_____

MERCY CARES FOR THE LOST

Read this Scripture passage several times, slowly. Emphasize a different word or phrase each time you read the passage. Underline keywords or phrases that are especially meaningful to you. Then take a few minutes to write your thoughts on the journal page. Finish with a prayer.

We should all be concerned about our neighbor and the good things that will build his faith.

ROMANS 15:2 (GW)

WHAT DID YOU HEAR?

What did God say to you as you read today's Bible passage? What word or phrase was most meaningful to you?

WHAT DO YOU THINK?

What does this passage mean to you? How does it apply to your life?

WHAT WILL YOU DO?

How will you put this verse into practice?

NOW YOU PRAY

This is where you turn your thoughts into prayer. It could be a prayer of gratitude or praise. It could be a prayer of confession or a request for God's help. It's up to you. But take a minute to write a prayer of response to God.

MERCY CARES FOR THE LOST

Read this Scripture passage several times, slowly. Emphasize a different word or phrase each time you read the passage. Underline keywords or phrases that are especially meaningful to you. Then take a few minutes to write your thoughts on the journal page. Finish with a prayer.

It's not important who does the planting, or who does the watering. What's important is that God makes the seed grow. The one who plants and the one who waters work together with the same purpose. And both will be rewarded for their own hard work.

1 CORINTHIANS 3:7–8 (NLT[2005])

WHAT DID YOU HEAR?

What did God say to you as you read today's Bible passage? What word or phrase was most meaningful to you?

WHAT DO YOU THINK?

What does this passage mean to you? How does it apply to your life?

WHAT WILL YOU DO?

How will you put this verse into practice?

NOW YOU PRAY

This is where you turn your thoughts into prayer. It could be a prayer of gratitude or praise. It could be a prayer of confession or a request for God's help. It's up to you. But take a minute to write a prayer of response to God.

MERCY CARES FOR THE LOST

Read this Scripture passage several times, slowly. Emphasize a different word or phrase each time you read the passage. Underline keywords or phrases that are especially meaningful to you. Then take a few minutes to write your thoughts on the journal page. Finish with a prayer.

Be wise in the way you act toward outsiders; make the most of every opportunity.

COLOSSIANS 4:5 (NIV)

WHAT DID YOU HEAR?

What did God say to you as you read today's Bible passage? What word or phrase was most meaningful to you?

WHAT DO YOU THINK?

What does this passage mean to you? How does it apply to your life?

WHAT WILL YOU DO?

How will you put this verse into practice?

NOW YOU PRAY

This is where you turn your thoughts into prayer. It could be a prayer of gratitude or praise. It could be a prayer of confession or a request for God's help. It's up to you. But take a minute to write a prayer of response to God.

SMALL GROUP
RESOURCES

HELPS FOR HOSTS

TOP TEN IDEAS FOR NEW HOSTS

CONGRATULATIONS! As the host of your small group, you have responded to the call to help shepherd Jesus' flock. Few other tasks in the family of God surpass the contribution you will be making. As you prepare to facilitate your group, whether it is one session or the entire series, here are a few thoughts to keep in mind.

- Remember you are not alone. God knows everything about you, and he knew you would be asked to facilitate your group. Even though you may not feel ready, this is common for all good hosts. God promises, *"I will never leave you; I will never abandon you"* (Hebrews 13:5 TEV). Whether you are facilitating for one evening, several weeks, or a lifetime, you will be blessed as you serve.

- Don't try to do it alone. Pray right now for God to help you build a healthy team. If you can enlist a co-host to help you shepherd the group, you will find your experience much richer. This is your chance to involve as many people as you can in building a healthy group. All you have to do is ask people to help. You'll be surprised at the response.

- Be friendly and be yourself. God wants to use your unique gifts and temperament. Be sure to greet people at the door with a big smile ... this can set the mood for the whole gathering. Remember, they are taking as big a step to show up at your house as you are to host a small group! Don't try to do things exactly like another host; do them in a way that fits you. Admit when you don't have an answer and apologize when you make a mistake. Your group will love you for it and you'll sleep better at night.

- Prepare for your meeting ahead of time. Preview the session and write down your responses to each question.

- Pray for your group members by name. Before your group arrives, take a few moments to pray for each member by name. You may want to review the *Small Group Prayer* and *Praise Report* at least once a week. Ask God to use your time together to touch the heart of each person in your group. Expect God to lead you to whomever he wants you to encourage or challenge in a special way. If you listen, God will surely lead.

- When you ask a question, be patient. Someone will eventually respond. Sometimes people need a moment or two of silence to think about the question. If silence doesn't bother you, it won't bother anyone else. After someone responds, affirm the response with a simple "thanks" or "great answer." Then ask, "How about somebody else?" or "Would someone who hasn't shared like to add anything?" Be sensitive to new people or reluctant members who aren't ready to say, pray, or do anything. If you give them a safe setting, they will blossom over time. If someone in your group is a wallflower who sits silently through every session, consider talking to them privately and encouraging them to participate. Let them know how important they are to you—that they are loved and appreciated, and that the group would value their input. Remember, still water often runs deep.

- Provide transitions between questions. Ask if anyone would like to read the paragraph or Bible passage. Don't call on anyone, but ask for a volunteer, and then be patient until someone begins. Be sure to thank the person who reads aloud.

- Break into smaller groups occasionally. With a greater opportunity to talk in a small circle, people will connect more with the study, apply more quickly what they're learning, and ultimately get more out of their small group experience. A small circle also encourages a quiet person to participate and tends to minimize the effects of a more vocal or dominant member.

- Small circles are also helpful during prayer time. People who are unaccustomed to praying aloud will feel more comfortable trying it with just two or three others. Also, prayer requests won't take as much time, so circles will have more time to actually pray. When you gather back with the whole group, you can have one person from each circle briefly update everyone on the prayer requests from their subgroups. The other great aspect of subgrouping is that it fosters leadership development. As you ask people in the group to facilitate discussion or to lead a prayer circle, it gives them a small leadership step that can build their confidence.

- Rotate facilitators occasionally. You may be perfectly capable of hosting each time, but you will help others grow in their faith and gifts if you give them opportunities to host the group.

- One final challenge (for new or first-time hosts). Before your first opportunity to lead, look up each of the six passages listed below. Read each one as a devotional exercise to help prepare you with a shepherd's heart. Trust us on this one. If you do this, you will be more than ready for your first meeting.

"When Jesus saw the crowds, he had compassion on them, because they were harassed and helpless, like sheep without a shepherd. Then he said to his disciples, 'The harvest is plentiful but the workers are few. Ask the Lord of the harvest, therefore, to send out workers into his harvest field.'"
MATTHEW 9:36–38 (NIV)

"I am the good shepherd; I know my sheep and my sheep know me—just as the Father knows me and I know the Father—and I lay down my life for the sheep."
JOHN 10:14–15 (NIV)

"Be shepherds of God's flock that is under your care, serving as overseers—not because you must, but because you are willing, as God wants you to be; not greedy for money, but eager to serve; not lording it over those entrusted to you, but being examples to the flock. And when the Chief Shepherd appears, you will receive the crown of glory that will never fade away."
1 PETER 5:2–4 (NIV)

"If you have any encouragement from being united with Christ, if any comfort from his love, if any fellowship with the Spirit, if any tenderness and compassion, then make my joy complete by being like-minded, having the same love, being one in spirit and purpose. Do nothing out of selfish ambition or vain conceit, but in humility consider others better than yourselves. Each of you should look not only to your own interests, but also to the interests of others. Your attitude should be the same as that of Jesus Christ."
PHILIPPIANS 2:1–5 (NIV)

"Let us hold unswervingly to the hope we profess, for he who promised is faithful. And let us consider how we may spur one another on toward love and good deeds. Let us not give up meeting together, as some are in the habit of doing, but let us encourage one another—and all the more as you see the Day approaching."
HEBREWS 10:23–25 (NIV)

"But we were gentle among you, like a mother caring for her little children. We loved you so much that we were delighted to share with you not only the Gospel of God but our lives as well, because you had become so dear to us. . . . For you know that we dealt with each of you as a father deals with his own children, encouraging, comforting and urging you to live lives worthy of God, who calls you into his kingdom and glory."
1 THESSALONIANS 2:7–8, 11–12 (NIV)

FREQUENTLY ASKED QUESTIONS

HOW LONG WILL THIS GROUP MEET?

This study is six sessions long. We encourage your group to add a seventh session for a celebration. In your final session, each group member may decide if he or she desires to continue on for another study. At that time you may also want to do some informal evaluation, discuss your Small Group Guidelines (see page 153), and decide which study you want to do next. We recommend you visit our website at *rickwarren.org* for more video-based small-group studies.

WHO IS THE HOST?

The host is the person who coordinates and facilitates your group meetings. In addition to a host, we encourage you to select one or more group members to lead your group discussions. Several other responsibilities can be rotated, including refreshments, prayer requests, worship, or keeping up with those who miss a meeting. Shared ownership in the group helps everybody grow.

WHERE DO WE FIND NEW GROUP MEMBERS?

Recruiting new members can be a challenge for groups, especially new groups with just a few people, or existing groups that lose a few people along the way. We encourage you to use the *Circles of Life* diagram on page 155 of this study guide to brainstorm a list of people from your workplace, church, school, neighborhood, family, and so on. Then pray for the people on each member's list. Allow each member to invite several people from their list. Some groups fear that newcomers will interrupt the intimacy that members have built over time. However, groups that welcome newcomers generally gain strength with the infusion of new blood. Remember, the next person you add just might become a friend for eternity. Logistically, groups find different ways to add members. Some groups remain permanently open, while others choose to open periodically, such as at the beginning or end of a study. If your group becomes too large for easy, face-to-face conversations, you can subgroup, forming a second discussion group in another room.

HOW DO WE HANDLE THE CHILD-CARE NEEDS IN OUR GROUP?

Child-care needs must be handled very carefully. This is a sensitive issue. We suggest you seek creative solutions as a group. One common solution is to have the adults meet in the living room and share the cost of a baby sitter (or two) who can be with the kids in another part of the house. Another popular option is to have one home for the kids and a second home (close by) for the adults. If desired, the adults could rotate the responsibility of providing a lesson for the kids. This last option is great with school-age kids and can be a huge blessing to families.

SMALL GROUP GUIDELINES

It's a good idea for every group to put words to their shared values, expectations, and commitments. Such guidelines will help you avoid unspoken agendas and unmet expectations. We recommend you discuss your guidelines during Session One in order to lay the foundation for a healthy group experience. Feel free to modify anything that does not work for your group.

We agree to the following values:

CLEAR PURPOSE	To grow healthy spiritual lives by building a healthy small group community
GROUP ATTENDANCE	To give priority to the group meeting (call if I am absent or late)
SAFE ENVIRONMENT	To create a safe place where people can be heard and feel loved (no quick answers, snap judgments, or simple fixes)
BE CONFIDENTIAL	To keep anything that is shared strictly confidential and within the group
CONFLICT RESOLUTION	To avoid gossip and to immediately resolve any concerns by following the principles of Matthew 18:15–17
SPIRITUAL HEALTH	To give group members permission to speak into my life and help me live a healthy, balanced spiritual life that is pleasing to God
LIMIT OUR FREEDOM	To limit our freedom by not serving or consuming alcohol during small group meetings or events so as to avoid causing a weaker brother or sister to stumble (1 Corinthians 8:1–13; Romans 14:19–21)
WELCOME NEWCOMERS	To invite friends who might benefit from this study and warmly welcome newcomers
BUILDING RELATIONSHIPS	To get to know the other members of the group and pray for them regularly
OTHER	_____ _____ _____

We have also discussed and agree on the following items:

- Child Care _____

- Starting Time _____

- Ending Time _____

If you haven't already done so, take a few minutes to fill out the *Small Group Calendar* on page 158.

CIRCLES OF LIFE

DISCOVER WHO YOU CAN CONNECT IN COMMUNITY

Use this chart to help carry out one of the values in the *Small Group Guidelines,* to "Welcome Newcomers."

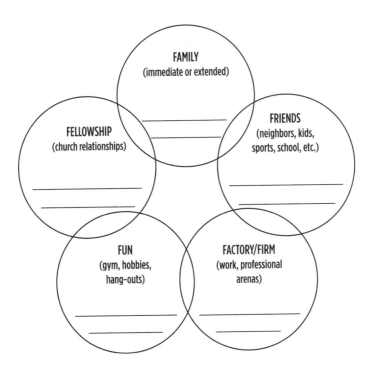

FOLLOW THIS SIMPLE THREE-STEP PROCESS:

1. List one to two people in each circle.

2. Prayerfully select one person or couple from your list and tell your group about them.

3. Give them a call and invite them to your next meeting. Over fifty percent of those invited to a small group say, "Yes!"

SMALL GROUP PRAYER AND PRAISE REPORT

This is a place where you can write each other's requests for prayer. You can also make a note when God answers a prayer. Pray for each other's requests. If you're new to group prayer, it's okay to pray silently or to pray by using just one sentence:

"God, please help _____ to
_____."

DATE	PERSON	PRAYER REQUEST	PRAISE REPORT

DATE	PERSON	PRAYER REQUEST	PRAISE REPORT

SMALL GROUP CALENDAR

Healthy groups share responsibilities and group ownership. It might take some time for this to develop. Shared ownership ensures that responsibility for the group doesn't fall to one person. Use the calendar to keep track of social events, mission projects, birthdays, or days off. Complete this calendar at your first or second meeting. Planning ahead will increase attendance and shared ownership.

DATE	LESSON	LOCATION	FACILITATOR	SNACK OR MEAL
	SESSION 1			
	SESSION 2			
	SESSION 3			
	SESSION 4			
	SESSION 5			
	SESSION 6			

ANSWER KEY

SESSION ONE

- Mercy is <u>LOVE</u> in <u>ACTION</u>.
- I <u>FORGIVE</u> those who have <u>FALLEN</u>.
- I <u>HELP</u> those who are <u>HURTING</u>.
- I am <u>PATIENT</u> with difficult people.
- I am <u>KIND</u> to my <u>ENEMIES</u>.
- I <u>CARE</u> for the <u>LOST</u>.
- I must be merciful because <u>GOD IS MERCIFUL</u>.
- I must be merciful because <u>I NEED MERCY EVERY DAY</u>.
- I must be merciful because <u>MERCY MAKES ME HAPPY</u>.

SESSION TWO

- Because <u>GOD HAS FORGIVEN ME</u>.
- Because <u>RESENTMENT MAKES ME MISERABLE</u>.
- Because <u>I WILL NEED FORGIVENESS</u> in the future.
- <u>LEAVE IT TO GOD</u>.
- <u>HEAL IT WITH GRACE</u>.
- <u>NAIL IT TO THE CROSS</u>.

SESSION THREE

- I keep my <u>DISTANCE</u>.
- I'm curious but <u>UNINVOLVED</u>.
- I get close enough to <u>CARE</u>.
- I must <u>SEE THE NEEDS</u> of people around me.
- I must <u>SYMPATHIZE</u> with people's pain.
- I must <u>SEIZE THE MOMENT</u> and meet the need.
- I must <u>SPEND</u> whatever it takes.

SESSION FOUR

- LOOK BEHIND THEIR BEHAVIOR.
- REFUSE TO BE OFFENDED.
- CUT THEM SOME SLACK.
- REFUSE TO GOSSIP ABOUT THEM.
- REFUSE TO PLAY THEIR GAME.
- ALWAYS TAKE THE HIGH GROUND.

SESSION FIVE

1. MAKE THE FIRST MOVE.
2. ASK GOD FOR WISDOM.
3. START WITH YOUR OWN CONFESSION.
4. LISTEN TO THEIR PAIN AND PERSPECTIVE.
5. SPEAK THE TRUTH TACTFULLY.
6. FIX THE PROBLEM, NOT THE BLAME.
7. FOCUS ON RECONCILIATION, NOT RESOLUTION.

SESSION SIX

- The Principle of COMPASSION.
- The Principle of COOPERATION.
- The Principle of FAITH.
- The Principle of ACTION.
- The Principle of PERSISTENCE.

SMALL GROUP ROSTER

NAME	PHONE	EMAIL
1.		
2.		
3.		
4.		
5.		
6.		
7.		
8.		
9.		
10.		
11.		
12.		
13.		
14.		
15.		

NOTES

NOTES

NOTES

NOTES

NOTES

NOTES

NOTES